Just for Laughs

TASTEFULLY SILLY JOKES ABOUT FOOD

Julia Garstecki

BLACK RABBIT BOOKS

Hi Jinx is published by Black Rabbit Books
P.O. Box 227, Mankato, Minnesota, 56002.
www.blackrabbitbooks.com
Copyright © 2022 Black Rabbit Books

Marysa Storm, editor; Michael Sellner, designer
and photo researcher

Library of Congress Cataloging-in-Publication Data
Names: Garstecki, Julia, author.
Title: Tastefully silly jokes about food /
by Julia Garstecki.
Description: Mankato, Minnesota :
Black Rabbit Books, [2022] | Series: Hi jinx.
Just for laughs | Includes bibliographical references
and index. | Audience: Ages: 8-12 | Audience: Grades: 4-6 |
Summary: "Through an engaging design that brings the
jokes to life with fun facts and critical thinking questions,
Tastefully Silly Jokes about Food will have readers
laughing and learning"– Provided by publisher.
Identifiers: LCCN 2020016600 (print) |
LCCN 2020016601 (ebook) |
ISBN 9781623107086 (hardcover) |
ISBN 9781644665633 (paperback) | I
SBN 9781623107147 (ebook)
Subjects: LCSH: Food–Juvenile humor. |
Food–Juvenile literature.
Classification: LCC PN6231.F66 G37 2022 (print) |
LCC PN6231.F66 (ebook) | DDC 818/.602–dc23
LC record available at
https://lccn.loc.gov/2020016600
LC ebook record available at
https://lccn.loc.gov/2020016601

Image Credits

123RF: shock77, 11; iStock: CandO_Designs, 18;
Westamult, 17; Shutterstock: anfisa focusova, 4;
Angeliki Vel, 19; Artisticco, 16; Big Boy, 6, 14, 16;
BlueRingMedia, 17; Denis Cristo, 20; Christos Georghiou, 4;
Dreamcreation, 3, 12; Ellagrin, 11; graphicgeoff, 10; GraphicsRF.
com, 1, 5; Hari_Aprianto, Cover, 5, 9, 23; Jamesbin, 15;
Kong Vector, Cover, 3, 6, 8, 9, 11, 12, 16, 18, 23; Konstantin
Alekseev, 18; Lorelyn Medina, 7, 13; Melok, 14–15; Memo
Angeles, 7, 8, 14, 15, 18–19, 19, 21; Nearbirds, 3, 12; Pasko
Maksim, 7, 14, 23, 24; Petrovic Igor, 6; picoStudio, 8, 9; Pitju,
19, 21; Reginast777, 7; Ron Dale, 5, 6, 10, 16, 20; rwgusev, 11;
stockakia, 2–3, 7; Tony Oshlick, 1, 13; Tueris, 16; Urip Junoes,
18; Vector Tradition, Cover, 4, 15; VizRad, 6; Yayayoyo, 13; your,
7, Yurlick, 16

CONTENTS

Chapter 1
Cheesy, Corny Jokes

Telling food jokes is like eating potato chips. Once you start, it's nearly impossible to stop. These cereal-sly funny jokes will have people hungry for more! Until they're full of laughter, that is!

Chapter 2
Snacks and APPS

How do salads say **grace**?

"Lettuce pray."

What's a computer's

favorite snack?

microchips

Fun Fact

One of the world's hottest peppers is the Carolina reaper.
A man once had to go to the hospital after eating one.

What does a
nosy pepper do?
gets jalapeño business

What kind of
bagel can fly?
a plain one

7

What is small, red, and whispers?

*a **hoarse** radish*

How much room is needed for **fungi** to grow?

as mushroom as possible

Why did the strawberry cry?

Because its parents were in a jam.

Chapter 3

Time for the Main Course

A taco and some
nachos were hanging out.
The nachos were sad.
The taco said,
"Wanna taco bout it?"
The nachos replied,
"It's nacho business."

What's a **matador's** favorite sandwich?

a bull-oney sandwich

What do you call a fake noodle?

an impasta

Why did the fettuccine run
from the haunted house?

It was too Alfredo!

What do you call a
frozen frankfurter?

a chili dog

What food
is always cold?

a brrrrrrr-ger

What should you eat if you're so
hungry you could eat a house?

wall nuts and cottage cheese

What should you do if
your soup is too hot?

Add a chilly pepper!

How do you turn
soup into gold?
*Put 14 **karats** in it.*

What did the taco
say to the burrito?
"Where you bean?"

Chapter 4
Delicious Dessert Jokes

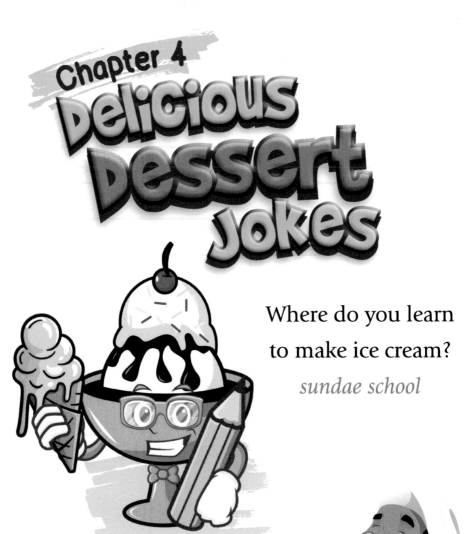

Where do you learn
to make ice cream?

sundae school

Why did the chef
open a bakery?

for the extra dough

Why did the students
eat their homework?
*The teacher said it
was a piece of cake.*

What kind of bear
has no teeth?
a gummy bear

17

Why did the cookie cry?
*Because its mom was
a wafer too long.*

Why did the pie
go to the dentist?
Because it needed a filling.

What do you call a cow that can't moo?

*a milk **dud***

What do you call a sheep
covered in chocolate?

a candy baa

Chapter 5
Get in on the Hi Jinx

If you enjoyed these food jokes, you might want to be a chef someday. There are many kinds of chefs. They specialize in different foods. Sauciers are in charge of sauces. Pastry chefs focus on breads and desserts. Rotisseurs cook and prep all the meat, and poissoniers make the fish. What kind of chef would you want to be?

Take It One Step More

1. What is your favorite food?
   Write three jokes about it.

2. What food has a weird or silly name?
   How can you turn that into a joke?

3. There are even more types of chefs.
   Do some research to learn
   about them.

GLOSSARY

civilization (siv-uh-luh-ZEY-shuhn)—
a well-organized and developed society
of people

dud (DUHD)—something that does not
do what it is supposed to do

fungus (FUN-gus)—a living thing, similar
to a plant that has no flowers, that lives on
dead or decaying things

grace (GREYS)—a short prayer at a meal

hoarse (HAWRS)—having a harsh or rough
sound or voice

karat (KAR-uht)—a unit for measuring how
pure a piece of gold is

matador (MAT-uh-dawr)—a bullfighter
who has the major part in a bullfight and
who kills the bull

BOOKS

Icuza, Vasco. *The A to Z Food Joke Book.* Tulsa, OK: Kane Miller, A Division of EDC Publishing, 2021.

Nickel, Scott, and Mark Acey. *Garfield's All-about-the-Food Jokes.* Garfield's Belly Laughs. Minneapolis: Lerner Publications, 2021.

Whiting, Vicki, and Jeff Schinkel. *Super Silly Jokes for Kids.* Mount Joy, PA: Happy Fox Books, 2020.

WEBSITES

Food Jokes: From Vegetable Jokes to Taco Jokes
www.rd.com/jokes/food-jokes/

Jokes for Kids: Big List of Clean Food Jokes
www.ducksters.com/jokes/food.php

Laugh Out Loud Funny Food Jokes for Kids
www.squiglysplayhouse.com/JokesAndRiddles/FoodJokes.php